SUMMARY of

HILLBILLY ELEGY

A MEMOIR OF A FAMILY AND CULTURE IN CRISIS

by J.D. Vance

A BriskReads Book Summary

Understand Main Takeaways & Analysis

The information provided in this book is designed to provide helpful information on

the subjects discussed. The author's books are only meant to provide the reader with

the basics knowledge of the topic in question, without any warranties regarding

whether the reader will, or will not, be able to incorporate and apply all the

information provided. Although the writer will make his best effort share her

insights, the topic in question is a complex one, and each person needs a different

timeframe to fully incorporate new information. Neither this book, nor any of the

author's books constitute a promise that the reader will learn anything within a

certain timeframe.

TABLE OF CONTENTS

EXECUTIVE SUMMARY

In Hillbilly Elegy, J.D. Vance offers an accurate and individual record of a culture battling in crisis. His stories, while riveting, consider how common laborers white Americans are in charge of their mishaps. Known as rednecks, hillbillies or white waste, these common laborers have been on the decrease for as far back as 40 years, and Vance endeavors to reveal the underlying reasons for this concealed tragedy. This story is about how it feels when your provincial and social classes break down. Especially when you were conceived with those types sticking around your neck.

What makes this diary mind blowing is that Vance joins request and research with his particular firsthand experience.

As a kid who experienced childhood in Ohio in a soil poor Rust Belt town, a significant number of his companions and associates feel that he had the extraordinary character to make it as an alum from the prestigious Yale Law School. The fact of the matter was that he was resolved not to surrender notwithstanding when he felt it is hard to proceed. It was enticing to offer into the financial misery that encompassed him. Destitution was prominent to the point that it had turned into a custom. Many people trusted that they could succeed just when they would do well to access to employments. However, Vance's perceptions investigate the genuine purposes behind their failure

INTRODUCTION

Vance's grandparents moved north to abandon their neediness and finish something in life. It was some time after World War II. They were pitifully infatuated, and despite the fact that they figured out how to walk along as a white collar class family, they likewise conveyed their Appalachian propensities and qualities with them. While some of them were certain attributes, different practices included verbal and physical mishandle that had nearly turned into their lifestyle. It was anything but difficult to trust that the lower and white collar class Americans were flopping fundamentally because of their monetary frailties, however as Vance kept on growing up, he adapted something else.

Savagery dug in itself in the family, and if it hadn't been for Vance's grandparents – Papaw and Mamaw – who accommodated and turned into his informal gatekeepers, life would have turned out to be fantastically intense for youthful Vance. In this hypnotizing journal, he additionally expounds on hopelessness, trust, and the group that points the finger at others for their particular mishaps. Vance, in his particular words, isn't an impartial spectator, and he maybe doesn't know every one of the appropriate responses. However, this book will without a doubt make you sit up and consider how people wind up where they do.

CHAPTER 1

Vance spent his youth in the residential community of Jackson, Kentucky. It was an excellent place that housed the kindest people with a profoundly inserted Appalachian culture. They regarded the dead and helped other people in need, yet they were likewise the kind of individuals who evaded work and rationalized everything.

Vance invested the greater part of his energy with his grandparents who protected him from the most exceedingly bad of his family. His Mamaw fundamentally guaranteed that he never saw any of his mom's show amid her occasional visits. The family moved to Ohio to escape all the bad habit and destitution, yet despite everything, he went by Jackson regularly to visit his old and incredibly weak grandma.

Jackson had many issues, and as though the destitution wasn't sufficient, the town started to battle significantly more when a medication fixation flourished. The training framework was bombing too, however with poor guardians without the advantage of a decision; they are compelled to send their children to the loathsome schools in any case. At the point when Vance was a little kid, he had a profound feeling of gratefulness towards the town and his family. Be that as it may, as he developed more seasoned, it was horrendously clear that the people were enduring just because they weren't making a move.

The people of Vance's childhood are mean and dither to open about their issues. In spite of the way that they can't bear the cost of treatment for even the most primary therapeutic care, they take the minor examination of it as an offense. They would prefer not to be judged, yet this line of thought has now pushed them to a place where they deny their issues. For example, when ABC highlighted the dental issues tormenting youthful youngsters in its report, local people reacted by disgracing ABC, asserting that the report was hostile and in an attack on their security.

A review directed on the neighborhood adolescents recommends that they dodge awkward truths from an incredibly young age. Rather than discovering answers for their squeezing issues, they imagine that a superior truth exists, which makes it practically inconceivable for them to gauge their circumstances with a clean, clear personality. With their judgment obfuscated, they build up a propensity to downplay and exaggerate while they overlook the negatives and laud the encouraging points in themselves.

Key Takeaways

The hillbilly culture instructs youngsters to disregard their issues at an incredibly young age. This creates as a propensity to make a 'substitute reality' as adolescents in which their problems don't exist.

This resistance system gives strength to hardship, additionally, makes it difficult to look at one self genuinely.

Rather than discovering answers for their neediness and other squeezing issues, they accuse others and avoid work notwithstanding when openings introduce themselves.

CHAPTER 2

In the midst of all the chaos that encompassed his life, Vance's grandparents bolstered him and showed him lessons most children gather from their folks. They did their best to guarantee that he had the absolute best to experience the American Dream, despite the fact that they seldom expected anything much from their lives. Mamaw wound up noticeably pregnant with Papaw's youngster when she was only 14; however, she lied about her age to keep any further inconveniences.

With an additional mouth to encourage, things searched inauspicious for the young couple, so they cleared out for Ohio at the earliest opportunity. Papaw worked at Armco – a steel organization that consistently employed candidates from Kentucky. As different families were relocating recently like them, they ended up in a natural situation, albeit still isolated from their more distant family. Notwithstanding being encompassed by numerous other

Kentuckians, issues proliferated from both finishes. While the people back in Kentucky anticipated that they would frequently visit (in spite of without the methods), the white Ohioans were suspicious of the Appalachian vagrants.

The Vance family did their best to change by their new way of life. They faced a couple of challenges. However, they realized that benefit and riches mattered an incredible arrangement in America. Middleton was far not the same as Kentucky, and they concentrated on their work and did everything conceivable to improve their lives.

Once in a while, they would show their Appalachian outrage when they couldn't bear that their kid was being abused. At the point when a store agent upbraided Jimmy for playing with an expensive toy, Papaw crushed the toy into pieces while Mamaw diverted random things from the racks, shouting obscenities. This dash of viciousness didn't trouble them at all since they genuinely trusted it was totally ordinary. It was dependably some portion of the hillbilly lifestyle.

Papaw chipped away at autos at whatever point he had sufficient energy to extra, and Mamaw did what she could to keep the family together. She longed for turning into a kids' legal advisor one day, yet she never sought after it as she had no chances to do as such.

As they had left Kentucky to think ambitiously, they anticipated that their kids would make utilization of the head begin they accommodated them.

Key Takeaways

Despite the fact that Vance's grandparents were poor, they did all that they could to guarantee that he had the best shot at accomplishing the American Dream.

Run of the mill hillbilly families is to such an extent that they'd preferably shoot at you than contend with you.

CHAPTER 3

Mamaw and Papaw had their first tyke – Jimmy – in 1951. They needed all the more, so they continued attempting even after Mamaw had nine unsuccessful labors. They chose to quit trying once they had three youngsters, in spite of the fact that Mamaw was profoundly scarred. Before long, however, one could see their marriage deteriorating primarily given Papaw's drinking propensity.

While Papaw was a fierce plastered who even punched Mamaw in the eye in an attack of fierceness, Mamaw was a savage nondrinker who once crushed a vase on her better half's brow. All things considered, they had great existences – Papaw earned well, and they were wealthier than the family they deserted in Kentucky. Be that as it may, within, they were going into disrepair. Mamaw's siblings, who were greatly defensive of her before marriage, were presently supporting Papaw in proceeding with his indecencies.

Mamaw figured out how to make companions, yet she started to pull back gradually to such a degree, to the point that the area kids regularly alluded to her as the "shrewd witch" on McKinley Street. The more Papaw drank, the more Mamaw disregarded the house, and a little while later, the rooms were necessarily overflowing with waste that had no esteem. In the midst of this, their hillbilly culture was more grounded than at any other time. The couple would keep quiet and go ahead with their lives apparently; however, it took little for them to wind up noticeably all of a sudden deadly. Mamaw despised unfaithfulness with such wildness that she thought of it as a cardinal sin with negative results to be distributed voluntarily.

As time cruised by, Papaw's hysterics proceeded, and he spent

the majority of his evenings drinking. Mamaw made it her life's

central goal to torment him utilizing her insidious means.

Fantastically, she even splashed his body with fuel and tossed a

match on his trunk since he'd returned home tipsy. They

proceeded with along these lines for quite a while until they

saw the implications.

Their kids, because of a harried youth with both Guardians

battling viciously, had issues when they became an adult. Lori

and Jimmy found their direction, yet Bev (Vance's mom) who

got pregnant when she was 18, wasn't so lucky.

Papaw quit drinking, and despite the fact that they now lived

independently, they fraternized. From helping Lori escape her

marriage to loaning cash to Bev for kid mind, they made every effort to help their youngsters. The couple who had fizzled

their children in their childhood had now devoted their lives to

compensating for it.

Key Takeaways

Most regular workers families live willfully ignorant and feel that they are ordinary regardless of the possibility that they can move from being quiet to lethal instant.

The hillbilly culture is a mix of respect, sexism, and reliability that occasionally turns into an explosive combination.

CHAPTER 4

As a tyke, Vance trusted that Middletown could be sorted into three geographic areas. The first was the zone where the rich dwelled, particularly the specialists. The second was the one where the soil impoverished people lived, for the most part, close Armco. The third was the range where Vance lived with his family, and it housed manufacturing plants and relinquished distribution centers. In spite of the fact that there wasn't a considerable measure of distinction between this zone and the one with the poorest, he may be needed to trust that they weren't too poor.

As Vance grew up, it was hard not to see the breaking down of Middletown, but progressive, happening directly before his eyes. Regardless of the town's excellence, it was conceivable to buy homes at disposable costs. This change occurred for the most part because of the rising populaces of the common laborer's whites who occupied neighborhoods with great destitution. Regardless of the possibility that the people needed to move, they more often than not couldn't bear to do as such since it cost so much cash. At last, the ones who could manage the cost of it cleared out the town and the people who couldn't be caught.

Armco later converged with Kawasaki, which implied that the Japanese organization was giving Armco another shot. Be that as it may, however, it gave employments to many people, it was underestimated by most in the town. The children once in a while considered getting to be steel laborers and this proceeds even today as the guardians don't need their kids to wind up steel specialists either. Like the others, they likewise need their children to seek after the American dream. However, the main issue is that they aren't willing to strive to accomplish it.

Advanced education doesn't hold a considerable measure of significance in their eyes, yet they long for accomplishing something important. Understudies don't lose rest over their reviews because there's nobody to reveal to them the amount it is important. Vance was once in a while reviled for his poor execution as he grew up and this careless disposition proceeds with today.

People visit about an industry and diligent work while being willfully ignorant of their apathy. Reports recommended that the common laborer's whites were working harder than their school taught partners, however as a general rule they discussed buckling down a great deal more than they did it.

Key Takeaways

Middletown was a perfect town amid the 1980s, however, after some time, it has blurred away with almost no to boast of.

The legislature empowers homeownership, yet for the vast majority of the inhabitants of Middletown, remains exorbitant.

CHAPTER 5

At the point when Vance was six, his mom changed his name
to delete his organic father's memory. In spite of the fact that
she couldn't seek an instruction, she was dedicated to it for
him. She celebrated when her child made a request to peruse a
book and volunteered to help him with his science ventures. At
whatever point Vance slacked in his school work, she advised
him that it was dependably a gift to get training.

While his mom showed him the standards of football, Mamaw
guaranteed that the kid knew how to battle. The implicit decide
was that he could never stir up some dust, yet it was alright to
begin one on the off chance that anybody mocked your family.
This wild safeguard of one's own was an individual

characteristic of the Appalachian people. Mamaw additionally gave him various tips to stand his particular ground on the off chance that he at any point got into a battle. This gave Vance the quality to protect himself and different casualties from classroom spooks. After an occurrence where he educated a domineering jerk, Vance never got into a fistfight again.

Naturally, Vance's grandparents were his closest companions, however one day, his mom and stepfather, Bob, chose to move to Preble County to make tracks in the opposite direction from Mamaw's consistent obstruction. Be that as it may, things turned out poorly arranged. Notwithstanding losing his wellbeing and battling with his reviews, Vance's injury because of the brutality at home was apparently starting to appear. His mother even took a stab at conferring suicide, and they were all of a sudden back in Middletown without his stepfather. Vance's mom got significantly more whimsical as time passed by, and didn't delay to hurt her youngsters. Things slowed to a point where Vance's grandparents were allowed guardianship, and he could visit his mom just when he did as such.

Key Takeaways

Moving to another place can't fix the endless loop of savagery and mishandle that is instilled in the Appalachian culture

Luckily for Vance, his mom and grandparents put stock in training, yet many other kids were coming from hillbilly families aren't that fortunate.

CHAPTER 6

The one thing Vance despised as a kid was the inquisitive inquiries concerning his kin. It was sad when he understood that Lindsay – the main "full" sister he thought he had – was additionally a relative. Adding to his wretchedness was the disarray on father figures. As his mom changed men much of the time after Bob – Vance's legal father – separated her, he'd gradually understood that they were never intended to remain. His mom brought every one of these men into their lives for her reasons. However, she additionally needed somebody to deal with and cherish her kids. Toward the finish of everything, at an exceptionally young age, Lindsay and Vance touched base at the excruciating conclusion that they couldn't rely on upon anybody.

As of right now, Vance's mom felt that Bob could no longer take the weight of an extra kid, as Vance's organic father – Don Bowman – returned into his life. Incidentally, his mom had invested energy with various men looking for a father for her youngster, at the end of the day, she backpedaled to his organic father. In the wake of going through a couple of days with Don, Vance understood that his dad had improved. He still contended with his better half, yet it was nothing contrasted with the savagery he saw at home.

Vance likewise comprehended why his dad had changed. In spite of the fact that Mamaw and the others felt that he was useful to no end, Don's religious contemplations had guided him towards a superior way in life. Vance still clutched the terrible recollections since Don had relinquished them, yet after understanding that he had done all that he could to get his guardianship, the torment subsided to some degree. It was right now that his dad's religiousness affected Vance. Pulled into outreaching religious philosophy, he felt a developing question towards different divisions of society.

Vance, inundated in his contemplations about religion, began to take a gander at things in an unexpected way. He started imagining that craftsmanship shows offended his confidence, and he abhorred gays trusting they were bound to go to hellfire. He some way or another even persuaded himself that he was gay.

Obviously, as a young man, Vance was truly quite recently searching for anything to trust in, and religion gave him that something. After Mamaw persuaded him that he wasn't gay, he could at last take in alleviation.

Key Takeaways

At whatever point brutal battles softened out up Vance's home, he was spared simply because Lindsay had the presence of a brain to protect him and call their grandparents.

Vance, and many youngsters experiencing childhood in slope nation family units, long for any structure or belief framework they can hook on to.

In spite of the fact that the Vance family once in a while went by chapels, they staunchly put stock in God, and Mama always felt that one needed to look after the family as it was their Christian obligation.

CHAPTER 7

Life proceeded with the same for Vance until tragedy struck

one day. At the point when Mamaw called him asking about

Papaw, he realized that something wasn't right. Papaw had

adhered to a schedule, and his occasions were predictable to

the point that it was incomprehensible for him not to contact

anybody. Afterward, Vance and his mom discovered Papaw

slumped in his seat. He was dead. The man who had been

significantly more than a father to Vance was presently gone,

and he admitted to the way that Papaw was the best father he at

any point had.

Every one of the individuals from the family lamented this

tragedy, yet they all prepared it in an unexpected way. Mamaw, who dependably set up an overcome front now appeared to be lost. Lindsay invested more energy hanging out with her companions to adapt to it. Be that as it may, the person who endured the most was Vance's mom. Her outrage issues surfaced like never before, and she couldn't appreciate why the others lamented for his passing.

She started snapping at others for the scarcest of their slip-ups, taking her animosity out on anybody and anything. In the meantime, she fell into a proper medication fixation. This left the youngsters with no other decision than to battle for themselves. Lindsay, known as the main genuine grown-up in the family, was just a secondary school graduate. Vance was still in the seventh grade, yet they by one means or another made it work.

The children depended on each other to deal with their issues as opposed to alarming Mamaw. Since Mamaw had spent a lot of her life overseeing some crisis, they no longer needed to weight her. They even went to recovery sessions with their mom to help her quit her fixation. However, it was a hard time for everybody included.

Vance's mom enhanced after some time, yet she attempted to persuade her youngsters that they shouldn't pass judgment on her since medication dependence was a malady.

Much the same as you couldn't control growth or some other disease, she couldn't control her substance manhandle either. This rationale didn't interest the children, yet they realized that she was doing her best to stop, and together, they helped her conquer it.

Key Takeaways

Papaw – the limited who was a protective figure to Vance –
was not the perfect grandparent, but rather he was all that
Vance and his sister had.

Not everybody experiencing childhood in Appalachian culture
had a good example like Papaw to swing to. His death left the
family in more prominent confuse than at any other time.

CHAPTER 8

As Vance turned 14, Lindsay got hitched to a man who treated her with the regard she merited. It was a cheerful minute for the family, and Vance couldn't have been more substance. Especially when Lindsay imagined a tyke inside only one year of her marriage. Now, Vance started to trust that things would change for the high. It was not intended to be. One day, his mom declared that he needed to move to Dayton to remain with her and her most recent sweetheart. Vance responded to this irately, and his mother even made him see a specialist. While at the advisor, Vance was frightened that any admission of his would send his mom to imprison. Thus he misled the expert keeping in mind the end goal to secure her instead of work through his issues.

Since Vance would not like to remain with his mom, he chose to stay with his father. Following a couple of days, he understood that he was simply not up to it. After spending excessively many days in the midst of grown-ups battling, slapping, and shouting, his father's home felt ordinary and impeccable to him. However, a feeling of instability disturbed him. He didn't know his dad all around ok to examine anything with him transparently. Thus he chose to backpedal home and remain with Mamaw.

Mamaw respected his choice and let him know unequivocally that he had a place there. In any case, it was evident to Vance that she was excessively slight and depleted, making it impossible to nurture an adolescent. In this way, he had no real option except to come back to his mom and Matt in Dayton. In spite of the fact that his mother and Matt didn't battle to such an extent, it was confident that the relationship was destined to fall flat. Staggeringly, Vance's mom declared one day that she'd be getting hitched to Ken, her manager. Inside of two days, they moved to remain with Ken and his two youngsters.

Once more, Vance ended up in a befuddled state. He battled with Ken's child which constrained his mom to take him back to Mamaw's home. Vance didn't understand it then. However, he was near his limit. With appalling evaluations and regular letters from the school about his nonappearance, he started to endure.

Key Takeaways

By misleading the advisor, Vance showed the run of the mill Appalachian estimation of savagely ensuring your family regardless of the results.

In the wake of going through his life loaded with savagery, medications and touchy battles at home, an exhausting, ordinary life seemed ideal for Vance, yet it was still out of his compass.

The constant moving of homes and schools and gatekeepers is standard for hillbilly families, and it leaves school-age youngsters at an extreme drawback.

CHAPTER 9

Vance's mom had battled with her addiction for a long time.

Vance's limit, be that as it may, was the point at which she

requested him to give her his pee so she could breeze through a

medication test. Against his desire, he went along when

Mamaw demanded so as to spare her little girl from the law at

the end of the day. Mamaw likewise required that Vance

returns to her home to remain with her for all time. It was

intense for Vance to continue ricocheting starting with one

house then onto the next and she trusted that she could deal

with him.

Vance acknowledged her choice, however, as usual, he couldn't

shake off the inclination that he was just a weight to her.

Mamaw was regularly hard on him, yet regardless of how she treated him, Vance making the most of his time with her. She reminded him continually about the significance of instruction. He didn't have the heart to disclose to her that he was near dropping out of school. Be that as it may, when Mamaw burned through $180 for his charting adding the machine, despite the fact that she couldn't manage the cost of it, it stirred something in him.

Abruptly, Vance started considering his schoolwork necessary. He went through three consecutive years with Mamaw, which was the defining moment of his life. His evaluations enhanced, and he likewise started making companions. Upon Mamaw's request, Vance additionally began working at a market. It was there that he saw how people controlled the welfare framework by purchasing sustenance and offering it at marked down costs.

It was deplorable for Mamaw and Vance to understand that their group in Ohio had similar issues they had endured those years in Kentucky. The yelling matches, youngster mishandle, avoiding work because of lethargy, and medication-related issues were excessively commonplace. They saw an example in the greater part of their lives, and simply like Mamaw, they had moved starting with one place then onto the next looking for a superior life. Each one of those issues had failed them even after they trusted they had gotten away. Vance asked why every one of these matters held on in their group, yet he additionally understood that while their funeral poem was a sociological one; the team, their confidence, and the brain science likewise mattered.

Key Takeaways

Vance's mom battled with her substance addiction. However, she gave him cash because she equated warmth with cash.

In spite of the fact that Mamaw was the best thing that at any point happened to Vance, he was humiliated to tell his friends that he lived with her since he didn't have a typical American family.

Regardless of his shame, living with Mamaw in an unfaltering home for a long time permitted Vance to see the issues in his group for what they were.

CHAPTER 10

As Vance completed secondary school, he, in the same way as other of his companions, chose to set off for college. He additionally built up enthusiasm for golf – the rich man's diversion – and despite the fact that he didn't make it in the group, he delighted in playing with the ones who made it. Notwithstanding the fact that Mamaw didn't have the cash to help Vance seek after golf, she helped him discover old clubs since she realized that it would help him make wealthier companions. As he contemplated settling on choices about his future, he always stressed about whether he had the coarseness to complete.

In the wake of scoring great on the SAT exams, Vance chose to settle with either Miami University or Ohio State. Despite the fact that it was enchanting and energizing to get into a school, he was ignorant regarding the entire procedure. That was the point at which his cousin proposed that he enroll in the Marine Corps. They had a notoriety for molding young men into men, and Vance felt that was something he required. After a ton of thought, Vance chose that his nation needed his administrations. Mamaw was totally against his choice, yet after he had cleared out for training camp, her letters and love gave him the genuinely necessary bolster never to stop.

The preparation was unforgiving, yet Vance amazed himself by doing things he regarded incomprehensible. After he had returned home, he saw that everyone, including people he'd known for a considerable length of time, treated him with more respect. Before long, Mamaw's wellbeing disintegrated, and she slipped into a state of extreme lethargy. She passed away, yet for Vance, it was more than losing a mother. She was the one individual who had trusted that he could accomplish anything he needed. That much conviction, with the preparation he got in the Corps, changed his point of view on life.

More than anything, Vance discovered that he had thought little of his actual quality. Ideal from guaranteeing that he trim his hair short, to settling on an informed choice about a credit, the Corps showed him how to lead a satisfying life as a grown-up. He figured out how to inspire himself past continuance. Apparently, he likewise understood that regardless of the amount we disclose to ourselves that our decisions don't make a difference, they do.

Key Takeaways

Joining the Marine Corps gave Vance the viewpoint to perceive what he was fit for in life.

For some slope people who never leave the nation, they can't pick up that perspective throughout their whole lives.

CHAPTER 11

Vance started going to Ohio State University in 2007. He made many companions, yet simply like him, every one of his companions had lived in little Ohio towns and moved out with no enthusiasm for backpedaling. He had for the longest time been itching to be an attorney, so working at the Ohio Senate held a significant amount of claim. It permitted him to get a look into legislative issues he didn't exactly get it. His occupation helped him the profit. However, it wasn't sufficient to cover his obligations. Vance loathed obligation so much that he chose to work at a not-for-profit association and give his plasma to profit.

Only a couple of years prior, he had been a kid who was startled of heading off to college. Be that as it may, the Marine Corps had given him a feeling of strength where he juggled reviews, two occupations, and furthermore played around with his companions in the meantime. He took up another employment to pay for his healing facility bills when he developed wiped out, yet then needed to drop the Senate work since it paid the minimum. Vance adored the employment; be that as it may, he persuaded himself that he could take up something he delighted in later. The prizes were without a doubt going to come later.

Finally, following quite a while of juggling disease, his reviews, and different employments, Vance graduated. He backpedaled to remain with Aunt Wee in Middletown since she had accepted the part of the female family authority after Mamaw's demise. He likewise invested some energy with his mom. Indeed, even after such a variety of years, he just couldn't feel safe with her.

After graduating, Vance understood that he had an incredible energy and he couldn't stop. His confidence for the future made him perceive that he had every one of the open doors and apparatuses required to succeed. Be that as it may, people around him continued as before. The average worker's whites still had similar objections, issues, and lethargy in their lives. Vance was glad, because of his hopeful standpoint, however shockingly, that very state of mind made him an outsider among his particular people.

Key Takeaways

Most wealthy children either moved toward becoming

architects or specialists, yet Vance wasn't occupied with that.

Only the fact that he had a heading in his life fulfilled him

colossally.

Returning home after college refined the photo of lethargy and

dissent that existed in the place where he grew up. He knew his

determination implied he was no longer one of them.

CHAPTER 12

Vance had accepted that all legal counselors profited. Thus he

connected to Yale and Harvard. He didn't know about it, yet

when he got a call expressing that he was acknowledged, he

couldn't contain his delight. Yale was a very different place

than he'd at any point envisioned. Not exclusively did the

teachers urge understudies to pursue their enthusiasm, yet not

at all like other top schools, they likewise made it clear that the

understudies needn't stress excessively over their evaluations.

Yale was extraordinary from multiple points of view, yet

Vance couldn't shake off the inclination that he didn't have a

place. A significant portion of his companions originated from

wealthy families where cash rarely postured issues, so he

unquestionably didn't have a place in that classification. Loaded with what society called the "elites," Yale's social customs were a blend of both expert and individual systems administration occasions. All things considered, Vance fit the bill consummately as a white, straight, confident, tall male, yet within, he had never learned about so of place his whole life.

While Vance felt that his particular life offered nothing energizing, his companions and educators discovered it inconceivable impressive. As Vance was the just a single from his family who had ever gone to school, a great deal less an Ivy League school, he felt awkward discussing it back in Middletown as well. Despite the fact that his life was heading in the correct course, he started pondering about inquiries that had stayed unanswered for a long time.

Key Takeaways

Once at Yale, Vance understood that he didn't have a place anyplace in the public eye: excessively poor for the elites, and too useful for Appalachia.

The way that his new companions and educators discovered his foundations intriguing made Vance address his upbringing and its significance to an ever increasing extent.

CHAPTER 13

Vance fell hard for a lady named Usha and Yale turned out to be more tolerable. When he went to a supper facilitated by Gibson Dunn, it was clear that it was a prospective employee meeting. As people arranged over mixed drinks and dinner, the questioners weren't occupied with accreditations and résumés, yet their social standing did make a difference. In straightforward terms, they were searching for candidates who could stand their ground in a court.

Toward the finish of the supper, everyone, including Vance had found employment offers. Vance was shocked with the way things had turned out for him. He was repelled each time he connected for work already, yet now he was getting offers speedier than he could even process them. A whole week of meetings made it clear to him that productive people played an entirely unique diversion.

While ordinary people sent in their résumés and trusted that they would land a position, productive people didn't take that course. Rather, they organized, messaged companions requesting favors, had their meetings set well ahead of time, and even turned into guardians who educated them about everything including the way they dressed, talked and conveyed themselves.

Vance took in this the most difficult way possible when he fouled up in a meeting, yet gratefully, one of his referrers had as of now put in a suitable word for him, and it spared him. Social capital was a principal asset to be utilized, and if not for Yale, Vance wouldn't have been taught about such a large number of things about which he was already unconscious. Aside from gloating rights, getting admitted to prestigious schools offered the significantly more significant number of advantages than one could understand.

Key Takeaways

Vance's "unpleasant" childhood implied he wasn't prepared and made for all the systems administration and interviewing that accompanies going to Yale.

The more dug in Vance progressed toward becoming in the group at Yale, the more he understood and procured the benefits of having a place with a higher social class.

CHAPTER 14

Everything appeared to be impressive for Vance, and with his excellent sweetheart life was solid. In any case, there were a couple of signs that something was awry. At whatever point Vance couldn't help contradicting Usha, he considered just two choices: he could either pull back from it or enjoy a yelling match. Since the last didn't speak to him, particularly after he'd spent a decent piece of his life seeing battles in his hillbilly family, he felt it was ideal to flee from it. He additionally perceived that he was acting quite recently like his mom. His greatest dread that he would turn out like her appeared to work out.

Vance considered setting off to a clinician, yet he just couldn't force himself to discuss his issues with an outsider. Gratefully, the books he read offered a considerable measure of understanding, and he understood that he was experiencing what the analysts would name as ACEs – unfriendly youth encounters.

Irritatingly, Vance additionally recognized that while many people experienced ACEs, the common laborers had a higher rate. For example, when he gave a test to his Uncle Dan, Usha, Aunt Wee, and Lindsay to assess the adolescence injury they had confronted, Aunt Wee scored the most elevated with a 7, while he and Lindsay each scored a 6. As anyone might expect, Usha and Uncle Dan scored a zero since they hadn't encountered any youth injury.

Now, Vance started to study more about the ACEs, and his exploration demonstrated that youngsters were experiencing it not just had a higher danger of contracting tumor. However, they were additionally more prone to end up plainly fat, and to fail to meet expectations in any exercises they took up. Lindsay and Aunt Wee battled with their relational unions simply like Vance attempted to take a few to get back some composure on his feelings with Usha. They were alert constantly, and this helped Vance to remember his strikingly comparable conduct. Alongside this, notwithstanding, came the acknowledgment that not all things be damned. All he required was somebody to converse with – someone who comprehended him – and the more he contemplated getting to be plainly similar to his mom, the more he attempted to finally understand her.

Key Takeaways

Things were going awesome amongst Usha and Vance until she felt that he resembled a turtle who would withdraw into his shell at whatever point a contention happened.

The more Vance found out about unfavorable youth encounters, the more determined he was to understand how they influenced people all through adulthood.

CHAPTER 15

After moving on from Yale Law School, Vance wedded Usha, and they purchased a home in Cincinnati.

He landed a decent position and had accomplished the American Dream. In any case, different things continued as before. Despite the fact that he had sworn never to help his mom, he couldn't leave her, particularly when she required him. She had now taken up heroin, and however Vance would not like to let it be known, it finally appeared like she had no desire for a superior future. He doesn't avoid her any longer and does his best to help her, but at the same time, he's mindful of his confinements.

People frequently address Vance about taking care of the issues that exist in his group. Sadly, there's no such enchantment arrangement. For Vance to succeed, an excessive number of variables needed to become alright. While he saw numerous men go back and forth, he had Papaw as a father. Notwithstanding when his mom was exasperated, she ensured that he built up an affection for instruction, and in particular, he had Mamaw as a security net to guide him at whatever point he looked at her. Other people from the hillbilly group who have succeeded additionally concur with this. Their lives weren't flawless, yet they had good examples to help them amid desperate circumstances.

At the point when a gathering of business analysts discharged a review, it was apparent that while other parts of the nation had more open doors, poor children in the South, Appalachia, and the Rust Belt attempted to ascend in the levels of America's meritocracy. The financial experts likewise noticed that two critical components – pay isolation and single child rearing – prompted an uneven appropriation of chances.

Growing up with single parents who battle to deal with their youngsters can be extremely alarming for the tyke itself. Unless there's some person solid like Mamaw to deal with the child, it's extreme for the kid even to seek after a future. For Vance, he had Mamaw, Papaw, Aunt Wee, Uncle Dan and even his mom to help him, yet he concedes that if these people were to be expelled from the condition, he couldn't have wanted to be instructed, considerably less acquire a degree from a prestigious school.

Key Takeaways

Vance's prosperity depends on heap calculates that make it difficult to imitate for others.

The key string entwining different stories of hillbilly achievement is having good examples: without some level of strength and support, it turns out to be practically difficult to break the cycle of hillbilly lethargy and neediness.

One of the primary elements adding to the destitution and incident in the South, Appalachia, and theRust Belt is the unwillingness to perceive the reality of your circumstance and assume liability for your activities.

Thank You

For Reading

Made in the USA
Middletown, DE
28 June 2017